The Match Master

Andrea Almada and Jeanie Stewart
Illustrated by Becky Radtke

A Harcourt Achieve Imprint

www.Rigby.com
1-800-531-5015

Literacy by Design Leveled Readers: *The Math Master*

ISBN-13: 978-1-4189-3787-4
ISBN-10: 1-4189-3787-8

© 2008 Harcourt Achieve Inc.

All rights reserved. No part of the material protected by this copyright may be reproduced or utilized in any form or by any means, in whole or in part, without permission in writing from the copyright owner. Requests for permission should be mailed to: Paralegal Department, 6277 Sea Harbor Drive, Orlando, FL 32887.

Rigby is a trademark of Harcourt Achieve Inc.

Printed in China
1B 2 3 4 5 6 7 8 985 13 12 11 10 09 08 07

Contents

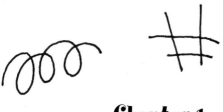

Chapter 1

All Finished!

Dora was so excited that she was the first student to finish the math assignment! She still had 15 minutes before going to gym class to play soccer. She looked at the math center and saw that Mr. Fong hadn't put out any new extra credit projects. Since she had already finished the ones that were there, she decided to read her library book.

Dora tapped her fingers impatiently, unable to focus on her book, as she watched the hands of the clock. She felt like time was moving at a snail's pace. *Finally* Mr. Fong announced that it was time to line up for gym. Dora leaped out of her seat and rushed to be first in line.

"Slow down, Dora," Mr. Fong said. "I know you're excited to play soccer in gym class. But you know that the rule is to wait until your group has been called to line up."

Dora slowly walked back to her desk and sank down in her seat. Lately it felt like she had to wait so long for everything she wanted to do.

Mr. Fong then called each group to line up, leaving Dora and Anthony's for last. As chairs squeaked across the floor and books were slammed shut, Mr. Fong said, "Dora, Anthony, I'd like to speak to you for a moment."

Worried, Dora hoped Mr. Fong wasn't still upset that she'd broken the class rule. But why did Anthony have to stay, too? Mr. Fong's knees bumped the desktop when he sat down next to Dora. Then he informed Dora and Anthony that because they had scored the highest on the practice test, they would represent their classroom in the fourth-grade math contest.

As they walked to the gym, Anthony teased Dora that he would soon be known as the fourth-grade Math Master, adding, "My dad and I are practicing together every night. Soon that medal will be hanging around my neck!"

"He's just jealous that you're going to win," Dora's friend Daisy said, and Dora silently hoped that Daisy was right.

9

Chapter 2

Back to First Grade

After gym, as the rest of the class finished the math assignment, Mr. Fong told Dora about a first grader named Beatriz who had recently arrived from Mexico. Although Beatriz was very smart, she was just learning English and was having trouble understanding some of her work. Since Dora could speak both Spanish and English, Mr. Fong thought she might be the perfect tutor for Beatriz.

"How would you like to work with her?" Mr. Fong asked.

Pleased that Mr. Fong trusted her with such an important job, Dora declared, "I'd love to help her!" After all, she often helped her younger brother Omar with his math homework, and he was a first grader, too.

"OK, since everyone else still has math to do, I'm sending you to Mrs. Moreno's classroom for the next 15 minutes."

"This will be fun!" Dora thought.

Mrs. Moreno welcomed Dora to the classroom and led her over to a little girl who was sitting at a table with three other first graders. Smiling, Dora said hello to Beatriz in Spanish, and Beatriz immediately grinned up at Dora as if she had found a long lost friend.

As Dora squeezed into a tiny chair beside Beatriz, her knees bumped the tabletop the same way that Mr. Fong had bumped his knees back in her classroom. It made her feel very grown-up. She opened the math workbook to the page Mrs. Moreno suggested and saw that it was just simple addition.

"OK, Beatriz, let's get to work," Dora said.

Beatriz nodded happily, but first she needed to sharpen her pencil. Then she wanted to sharpen all of her art pencils, and after that she showed Dora what she liked to draw with each colored pencil. Dora had expected Beatriz to be very shy and was surprised to find that Beatriz had a lot to say.

13

Dora was shocked when Mrs. Moreno announced that tutoring time was over. Beatriz's paper was covered with lots of squiggles and stars, but only three addition problems. Dora feared that Mrs. Moreno would think that Dora was a terrible tutor!

"I shouldn't have let Beatriz talk so much," Dora thought. "Tomorrow I'll have to be very firm, not let her chat or draw, and work with her until she gets everything done!"

Chapter 3

Tough Teacher

The next day, when Dora got to Mrs. Moreno's classroom, Beatriz handed Dora a rolled up piece of paper tied with blue ribbon and said in Spanish, "Dora, look at what I made for you."

Dora untied the bow and unrolled the paper to find a drawing of two girls who were holding hands, surrounded by red and pink hearts. Although they were just stick figures, the tall girl was clearly meant to be Dora, and the other was Beatriz.

"Come and see my pictures on the wall," Beatriz demanded, pulling Dora toward the art wall.

Flattered by her present, Dora wondered if any of those drawings were pictures of her, too. Then she reminded herself that she was the math tutor and should be helping Beatriz with her math, not looking at artwork.

Picking up a worksheet, Dora read aloud in English—and then explained in Spanish—a problem about adding oranges. Oranges reminded Beatriz of her uncle's farm in Mexico, and she whispered that she was homesick, tears filling her eyes.

Dora wished she could do something to cheer Beatriz up, but there wasn't time. Putting a finger to her lips, she ordered Beatriz not to talk until all of her math was done. Frowning, Beatriz started to work, and when her paper was filled with numbers, she shoved it toward Dora.

Dora began checking the problems, but six plus six was not six! Disappointed, Dora realized that the first problem was wrong . . . and the second problem . . . and the third. In fact, every problem on the paper was wrong!

With a deep sigh, Dora noticed that Beatriz was now happily drawing pictures of fruit on the next worksheet. Suddenly Mrs. Moreno announced that time was up.

Dora wanted to cry because she didn't feel like a Math Master. She was a failure—probably the worst tutor in the history of her school. She wanted to prove to Mr. Fong that she could be as good a teacher as he was.

For the next two days, Dora rushed through her own work so that she'd have more time for tutoring. She even gave up the time she'd planned to use studying for the math contest. Helping Beatriz became one of the most important things in the world to Dora.

Spending the extra time with Beatriz, in addition to being serious and not letting her talk so much, finally worked. On Friday Beatriz unhappily completed an entire addition worksheet without making a single mistake.

Dora left the classroom smiling proudly and looking forward to Monday when she would start teaching Beatriz subtraction.

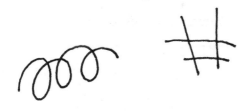

Chapter 4

A Number of Problems

Unfortunately, tutoring the next week did not go as well as Dora had hoped it would. When Dora tried to explain a subtraction problem by using pieces of macaroni, Beatriz just made macaroni patterns on the table. When Dora drew circles and colored in the ones to be subtracted, Beatriz colored in the rest. By Wednesday Dora was losing hope. How could Dora help Beatriz if Beatriz wouldn't work with her?

After school Dora marched over to Mr. Fong's desk and announced, "I can't do this anymore!"

Mr. Fong asked Dora to sit down and said, "Mrs. Moreno told me that you and Beatriz have not been getting along with each other very well lately. That doesn't sound like you, so what's wrong?"

Dora explained that Beatriz wouldn't do her work, even though the math problems were really easy.

"They're easy for you, but maybe they aren't so easy for a first grader. I know that Anthony is always calling you the Math Master, and to master a subject means to learn it well. That's a good thing, but sometimes when working with other people, it's better to be a *mentor* than a master."

Dora had no idea what a mentor was. Mr. Fong explained that a mentor was a trusted guide, like a friend who shared her knowledge. Dora said that she was already sharing her knowledge, wasn't she?

"You'll have to figure that out on your own, Dora, but I hope you won't quit."

Dora didn't want to disappoint Mr. Fong. However, she also didn't want to go back to the first-grade classroom ever again.

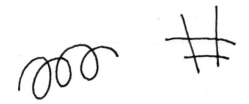

Chapter 5

Solutions

That night after dinner, Omar asked Dora for help with a math problem. Immediately she started to show him how to solve it, but he thought she was being bossy rather than helpful.

"Slow down! This is hard for me!" Omar cried.

"Well, it shouldn't be!" Dora snapped. "It's an easy first-grade problem, and you're just not listening to me."

Omar pushed the paper away and folded his arms against his chest.

"It's no wonder you're having trouble tutoring," Carlos said as he walked into the kitchen. "Maybe you should try to be nice instead of acting so mean."

Dora went to her room, slammed the door, and threw herself on her bed. Omar was acting just like Beatriz! How was she supposed to help anyone who just cried and gave up?

Suddenly she remembered the way she had gone to Mr. Fong and told him that she couldn't tutor anymore. She had sounded just like Omar, but there was one big difference: how Mr. Fong had acted.

Unlike Dora, Mr. Fong had been understanding and patient. He had listened to her instead of telling her that her problem was easy. He hadn't ordered her to fix her mistakes, and he had told her that he believed in her.

Dora wanted to be a good teacher like Mr. Fong, not the grouchy tutor she had become. She quickly went back to the kitchen and apologized to Omar. He was happy to be helped by her—once she stopped ordering him around and started encouraging him more. Soon he had finished every problem.

Dora felt much better and promised herself that tomorrow she would be Beatriz's math mentor instead of her grumpy tutor.

When Beatriz saw Dora the next day, Beatriz frowned and looked away. Dora apologized for being so impatient and asked for another chance. When Beatriz hesitated, Dora added, "We don't even have to do worksheets today because I brought a game."

Dora had brought her favorite game from when she was in first grade. It would make subtraction so much fun that Beatriz wouldn't even realize she was learning. Dora patiently explained the rules in English and in Spanish and she didn't even mind when Beatriz paid more attention at first to the game pieces—plastic, yellow circles—than to playing the game.

Before long both Dora and Beatriz were laughing and having a good time. Better yet, by the time Dora had to leave, Beatriz understood subtraction.

As Dora packed up the game, she noticed one of the circles was missing. However, she was in too much of a hurry to look for it.

Chapter 6

The Contest

The next afternoon, Dora, Anthony, and eight other fourth graders were waiting nervously on the stage for the math contest to begin. Beyond the closed curtains, Dora could hear noisy voices as the gym filled. Her heart was beating quickly, but she also felt good knowing that so many friends and relatives had come to watch.

"Good luck," she whispered to Anthony.

Instead of his usual teasing, Anthony replied quietly, "Good luck to you, too, Dora."

Mr. Fong crouched between their chairs and told Dora and Anthony that he was proud of them, then added, "Oh, Dora, Beatriz asked me to give you this." He handed her the missing yellow game circle, which had been threaded on a blue ribbon to make it into a necklace.

The principal approached the stage to start the contest. Dora shoved Beatriz's gift into her pocket, and Mr. Fong barely had time to leave the stage before the curtains slid open.

While the principal addressed the audience, Dora looked for her family and smiled when Beatriz, who was sitting in front of Omar in the first grade section, grinned and waved.

One by one, the students came to the front of the stage and answered a math question. When it was her turn, Dora put her trembling hand into her pocket and held on to the yellow circle. She answered her question clearly and correctly.

An hour later, only three students were left—Candace, Anthony, and Dora—and it was time for the speed race.

Chapter 7

And the Winner Is . . .

Three large chalkboards were rolled onto the stage where Dora, Anthony, and Candace would race to solve problems announced by the principal. The last person finished would have to leave the stage.

Even with her back to the audience, Dora could feel everyone watching. The principal had hardly finished saying the first problem before Dora's chalk was tapping across her board.

Finished, she spun around, but Anthony was already facing the audience! The principal and everyone else applauded as Candace, who finished last, left the stage. Dora solved the next problem as quickly as she could and spun around again . . . at exactly the same time as Anthony.

It was a tie, so the principal read another problem, but again they tied. Finally, on the next question the winner was announced . . .

37

"Good job, Anthony," Dora said as the principal presented him with the first-place ribbon.

As the principal hung a gold medal around Anthony's neck, Dora pulled the plastic yellow circle from her pocket and hung it around her own neck. She looked out into the audience and saw Beatriz beaming with pride. Beatriz could tell that Dora liked her present, especially when Dora smiled right at her. Then Dora turned to look at Anthony.

"You really are the Math Master," Dora said to Anthony.

"But you're still a Math Master, too," Anthony grinned back.

"Thanks, but you can call me Math Mentor from now on," Dora said, touching her plastic yellow medal. On it Beatriz had written something that Dora never wanted to forget: #1 Math Tutor!